Surviving College LIFE

Dealing with Studies, Stress, Love, Suicide, Mental Health, Alcohol, Drugs and More...

Written by: Dr. Stem Sithembile Mahlatini
Drstem14@gmail.com | www.drstemspeaks.com
https://www.drstemmie.com/
Facebook: DrStem Mahlatini
Twitter: DrStemahlatini
LinkedIn: Drstem Mahlatini
Skype: Dr.Mahlatini

Foreword by: Dr.Stem Sithembile Mahlatini
Cover Design by: Phillip Mudavanhu

Category: Historical, Biographical, Motivational, Inspirational,
Educational and Empowerment
Library of Congress Cataloging-in-Publication Data
Printed in the USA

Contents

Foreword

You're a College Student

Congratulations! You've successfully made it through high school and you're heading to college! The fact that you've come this far proves that you have what it takes to do anything you want to do in life. The sky is the limit for you.

Though this is an exciting time, it can also be a little intimidating because it's a completely different chapter in your life. Moving on to college means adapting to new friends, teachers (now referred to as professors), a new environment, and in many cases, a whole new way of life.

However, don't let that deter you from looking forward to what will be one of the most meaningful and memorable times of your life. College is a time for you to discover more about who you are as you continue to gain the knowledge and skills necessary to succeed in the world. You will have lots of practice exercising responsibility and accountability. You will also learn valuable lessons about dealing with people and maintaining relationships. Most importantly, you'll walk away with the necessary skills to pursue your career.

Adjusting to Being Away from Home

College life is a huge adjustment, so it's normal to have feelings of nervousness or even feel a bit overwhelmed at in the beginning. Once you become acclimated to the college environment and your new schedule, the adjustment will become much easier. There are several things you can do to prepare for a much smoother transition.

Preparing for The Move

If you're moving into a college dorm or apartment to be closer to campus, pack the bare essentials. Try not to overdo it by packing things that won't be of much use to you. Overpacking might be more of a hindrance if you're moving into a tight living space. For example, you'll only want to pack clothes for the current season if you live close enough to home to retrieve clothes for the next season. If you're moving far away, you can pack a few interchangeable outfits for each season. Of course, you'll also want to pack toiletries and bedding. It's also a good idea to pack a few things that remind you of home, whether it's a family photo or your favorite coffee mug.

Check with the college's student resident services about whether or not appliances are allowed, such as miniature refrigerators, microwaves, coffee makers, etc. Many campuses do not allow such appliances because they offer them in a communal setting. Some might even require you to pay a small fee to rent appliances. It's best to check with the college about what you should and shouldn't bring before spending money on items and packing them unnecessarily.

Maintaining Open Lines of Communication

There are several key people you'll want to remain in constant communication with once you're off to college, including your parents, student advisors, professors and Resident Life Director.

Your parents will want to know how things are going every step of the way—if you're safe and if you have everything you need along the way. You can reduce a lot of unnecessary stress between you and your parents by just checking in from time to time. It might not be possible to call every hour of every day because of your new schedule, but you should establish a time to call home at once or least twice a week, just to check in. This will alleviate your parents' worries and help prevent you from feeling home sick. If you'll be attending college within a reasonable driving distance, it's a good idea to set aside time to visit home when possible.

Your parents aren't the only people you need to remain in contact with. It's important that you also maintain an open line of communication with your professors. This might seem difficult to do because you're competing with the attention of other students. However, most professors keep an open-door policy or have designated hours when students can come by and talk with them outside of class hours. If you're unable to speak with your professors about something in person right away, email them or contact them using the college's online communication portal.

It's a good idea to introduce yourself to your professors early on so that you begin to establish a relationship with them. Let them know what your interests are and what you look forward to learning about most by taking their class. You can also share your strengths, weaknesses and what type of learner you are so that they are mindful of this when providing instruction and assigning projects.

You'll want to communicate often with your college registrar and student advisor. These are the people who will help guide you through which classes you need to take in order to complete requirements for a certain degree. They will also advise you on your progress throughout your tenure in college. For example, if you have questions about whether or not you have enough credits in a given semester or which courses are required, these are the people you'll want to talk to. Never leave your college status up to chance. Eliminate the guessing work by communicating with them as much as possible.

The same is true for financial aid. If you've taken out a student loan of any kind, your financial aid advisor is there to help guide you through questions about your payment status and how to apply for additional loans. We'll talk more about student loans in the next few chapters

Adjusting to a Foreign Country

Packing

If you're planning to attend college in a foreign country, preparation might be a lot different. For example, you might not be able to pack some of the same items you would for college in the states because there might be things that customs won't allow. Before you begin packing items for travel overseas, check with customs about required documentation and restrictions with regard to what you can bring.

Traveling overseas also means you'll be limited in terms of how much you can pack. In this case, it might be best to purchase larger items such as bedding and small appliances once you arrive to your destination. Be sure to check with the college about what is allowed into the living quarters before making purchases, just as you would in the states.

Language and Culture

If you are attending college in a country where the primary language is different than your native language, you'll need to become familiar with the native language of the country you'll be studying in. Even if you're not fluent, it will be important for you to understand basic words for everyday living. For example, you'll need to know how to introduce yourself to others, ask for directions and identify common foods. You'll also need to become familiar with the currency of the country if US currency isn't commonly used.

Being familiar with the culture of the country and community where you'll be studying is also important. You'll want to understand common gestures, body language, foods, slang and traditions. Understanding the culture can prevent you from feeling isolated from those in the community or misunderstanding the intentions of those you'll be sharing your college journey with.

Self-Reflection: Adjusting to Being Away from Home - Preparing for the Move

- Have you packed for your move to college?
- Is there anything you're unsure about in terms of what to bring?
- If so, write these items down and have a discussion with your parents and the college you plan to attend about whether or not they're necessary or allowed.

_____

_____

_____

_____

_____

_____

_____

_____

_____

_____

_____

_____

Self-Reflection: Maintaining Open Lines of Communication

- Have you and your parents talked about a communication plan?
- How often do you plan to check in with them by phone?
- How often do you plan to visit home?

_____

_____

_____

_____

_____

_____

_____

_____

_____

_____

_____

_____

_____

_____

_____

_____

_____

_____

_____

- Describe some of the interests, strengths and weaknesses you'd like to share with your professors. Also, describe what type of learner you are (i.e., visual learner, audio learner).

_____

_____

_____

_____

_____

_____

_____

_____

_____

_____

_____

_____

_____

_____

_____

_____

_____

_____

_____

_____

_____

Declaring a Major

If you've already identified a major for your degree, good for you! If you're still not quite sure about what area you want to focus on, that's ok, too! Many students enroll in college without knowing exactly which type of degree they want to focus on. As a result, they take several courses that interest them during their first semester, or even their first year, then decide which of their courses peak their interest most.

Some students decide to obtain a general studies degree, which is a degree that covers a broad range of basic college classes, including language arts, math and science. This program of study allows students to pursue careers in a wide variety of fields without specializing in one particular field of education.

If you already know what degree you want to pursue, make sure you check with the school registrar to confirm the classes you'll need to obtain your degree and develop a plan for which classes you want to complete each semester. Keep in mind that some classes are required as prerequisites for others, so you'll want to plan your schedule accordingly. You'll also want to registrar for your classes as early as possible, as some classes have space limitations and may become full.

Take some time to explore courses outside of your major, as well. Your first semester is a good time to take advantage of the opportunity to explore subjects of personal interest, especially if they count toward the credits you need. It is also a good idea to take courses that can provide you with additional life skills.

Many students opt to establish a minor in addition to their major. A minor is a declared discipline that is secondary to a major. Though a minor requires fewer college credits than what is required of a major—typically three years of courses, compared to four, a minor will require you to complete specific classes as criteria for completion. It is also possible to declare a double major or double minor. However, doing this might require extra hours or even an extra semester or two. Upon graduating, any completed majors or minors will be reflected on your student transcript.

Changing a Major

So, what if you want to change your major along the way? If you start down the track of a specific major but decide that it isn't for you, you can absolutely switch gears. In fact, you can change majors as many times as you'd like. Just be mindful that not all of the courses you've completed may be applicable to what is required of the new major you decided upon. This might also lengthen the amount of time it takes for you to complete your degree. However, if you're sure the major you initially declared isn't what you want to ultimately pursue, it's best to redirect before spending more time and money on obtaining a degree that you have no intention of using.

Try not to put too much pressure on yourself to declare a major right away if you're unsure. The good news is most of the core classes you'll be required to take during your freshman year will be applicable to any major.

If you hear a voice within you say 'you cannot paint,' then by all means paint and that voice will be silenced.

–Vincent Van Gogh

Self-Reflection: Declaring a Major

- Have you decided on a major?
- If so, what classes do you plan to take during your first semester?
- During your first year?

_____

_____

_____

_____

_____

_____

_____

_____

_____

_____

_____

_____

_____

_____

_____

_____

_____

_____

_____

_____

- If you have not decided on a major, what core courses are required of you?
- Aside from core courses, what other courses are offered that interest you most?

_____

_____

_____

_____

_____

_____

_____

_____

_____

_____

_____

_____

_____

_____

_____

_____

_____

_____

_____

_____

Believe in yourself and all that you are. Know that there is something inside you that is greater than any obstacle.

– Christian D. Larson

Online Courses

Most colleges and universities offer the flexibility of completing courses in-classroom and online. If you choose to take courses online, be sure to follow the same steps as you would when determining which courses to take in-classroom. You'll still want to know what is required and what the prerequisites of each class are.

You'll also want to know more about who is instructing the course and make it a point to introduce yourself online, if you're unable to do so in person.

There are pros and cons to taking courses online, also referred to as online learning. One of the biggest pros is flexibility. Taking courses online allows you to learn at your own pace and choose your own hours. It also allows the flexibility of learning anywhere, anytime. Online learning is also more individualized compared to in-classroom learning because you don't have to compete with learning among a large group of students.

If you're a fan of technology and social learning using platforms such as chat rooms, video chat and message boards, you might enjoy online learning.

Though technology can be a pro for some, it can be a con for those who struggle with it. Technology can also come with additional expenses, such as high-speed internet access, antivirus software and accessories/special features (i.e., microphone, camera). Other obstacles include time management and student engagement. Some students need the structure of in-person instruction to stay on task. Depending on your learning style, taking a class in-person and actively interacting with other students might also keep you more engaged than learning online.

Not all courses required to complete your degree might be online. It's important to talk to your academic advisor or school registrar about what is required and what your online options are.

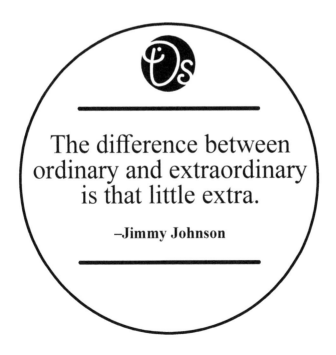

The difference between ordinary and extraordinary is that little extra.

–Jimmy Johnson

Self-Reflection: Online Courses

- Have you participated in online learning before?
- What was your experience?

_____

_____

_____

_____

_____

_____

_____

_____

_____

_____

_____

_____

_____

_____

_____

_____

_____

_____

_____

_____

_____

_____

_____

- Are you considering taking college courses online?
- Why or why not?

Student Loans

There are two types of loans available to students—private student loans and federal aid. Private student loans can be more difficult to obtain than federal loans because they require very good credit or a co-signer. They also tend to have higher interest rates than federal loans. Regulations and requirements for eligibility also differ based on the type of loan.

Stafford and Perkins loans are funded with government money and given directly to the student. These loans have low interest rates and can be consolidated upon graduation, which means you'll have the ability to combine several loans into a one loan for easier debt management.

There are two types of Stafford Loans: subsidized and unsubsidized. Subsidized loans are reserved for students who can demonstrate a financial hardship—typically an annual income of less than $50,000. If your loan is subsidized, you won't be responsible for making any payments until after you graduate because the government pays your interest for you while you're in school. Subsidized loan amounts vary based on what year you are in (i.e., freshman, sophomore).

If you have an unsubsidized loan, you're responsible for paying off all the interest but payments are typically postponed until after you graduate. Unsubsidized loans also typically have a larger range in terms of the loan amounts than subsidized loans.

Parent Loans for Undergraduate Students (PLUS loans) allow parents to take out loans for their children. Likewise, graduate students have access to Grad PLUS loans. Graduate students and medical students have access to higher limits.

If you're in need of a loan but you're unsure about what type of loan to apply for, talk to someone in the financial aid office at your college of interest. Your parents can also talk to someone at the branch where they bank about options for private loans. Regardless of the type of loan you decide on, keep in touch with your loan provider regarding questions you might have or changes in your circumstance along the way to ensure that your account remains in good standing.

There is no elevator to success. You have to take the stairs.

Zig Ziglar

Self-Reflection: Student Loans

- Are you considering applying for student loans?
- If so, do you know how much you need?
- Who do you plan to consult with about your loan options?

_____

_____

_____

_____

_____

_____

_____

_____

_____

_____

_____

_____

_____

_____

_____

_____

_____

_____

_____
_____
_____
_____
_____
_____
_____
_____
_____
_____

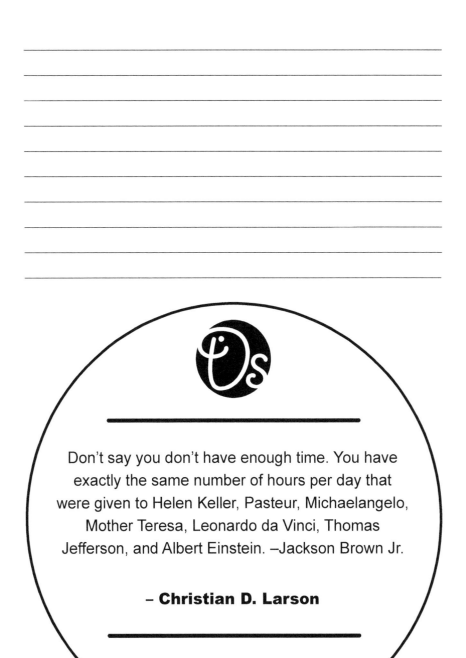

Don't say you don't have enough time. You have exactly the same number of hours per day that were given to Helen Keller, Pasteur, Michaelangelo, Mother Teresa, Leonardo da Vinci, Thomas Jefferson, and Albert Einstein. –Jackson Brown Jr.

– Christian D. Larson

Studying & Maintaining a Strong GPA

Now that you've made a financial commitment to completing a college education—regardless of how big or small, you want to make sure you get your money's worth by finishing strong. This will require lots of focus, dedication and, of course, studying.

Studying sounds easy enough but can be difficult for some because of competing priorities. You'll likely be taking several college courses at once, which means you'll need to devote time to studying each subject. In addition to your college courses, you might be involved in extracurricular activities and social groups on campus. Perhaps you'll even be working a part-time job. Not to mention, you'll also have a social life to maintain.

Be sure to set time aside for studying just as you would to watch your favorite television show or eat a meal. Don't be fooled by thinking attending class is all you need to do to inform your homework assignment, projects and help pass exams. Hearing instruction once will not help you retain the information. Studying helps to reinforce the information you learn in class so that you retain it better.

Did you know research shows that we retain 90% of what we learn by teaching someone else or using it immediately? Likewise, we retain 75% of what we learn by putting it into practice. This means it's not enough to simply sit in class or complete a lesson online and expect to retain it until weeks later, when it's time for an exam or project.

It's important to take notes daily and review them often. Don't procrastinate when it comes to studying. The more often you review the information, the easier it will be to retain it. Completing exercises, writing down study questions using what you've learned and reciting them often helps you to put what you've learned into practice.

Studying with a partner or group of students can also be greatly beneficial because it allows you to share what you've learned with one another as added reinforcement. Studying with others can also make studying fun, especially if you bore easily when studying alone.

The more you study, the higher your chances of achieving high grades on exams and assignments. This is important when considering your overall grade point average (GPA).

Much like high school, your GPA provides a standardized way for colleges to judge your academic merit. A common standard of satisfaction is a 3.0. However, the standard for GPA can be higher based on the college institution or declared major. Most colleges require students to maintain a 2.0 GPA to prevent being put on probation. A probationary period will require you to raise your GPA within a specified amount of time before being disenrolled due to failure to meet the school's standards.

Aside from remaining enrolled in good standing, maintaining a good GPA can provide you with great opportunities, such as invitations to honors societies, prestigious graduate programs, and a great-paying job. Many companies inquire about an applicant's GPA as part of their hiring process because they want to know how well you exceled in your degree.

Make sure you understand the GPA scoring system from the very beginning so that you are aware of how each letter grade will affect your GPA overtime. Your academic advisor can assist you with this.

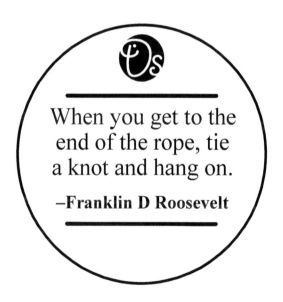

When you get to the end of the rope, tie a knot and hang on.

–Franklin D Roosevelt

Tips for Studying

- Take ample notes during class to assist you when studying.
- Study without distractions.
- Study in a comfortable and inviting environment.
- Set aside time to study each day.
- Divide study time so that you have dedicated time to focus on each subject area.
- Don't allow yourself to become overwhelmed. Take breaks.
- Highlight areas that you're having trouble understanding or remembering so that you can give them more focus each time you study.
- Refer to your textbook or study guide. They are there to help you.
- Don't be afraid to ask for help. Find a study partner or talk to your professor about areas that challenge you.
- Study with a group if you find it more engaging to study with others than studying alone.

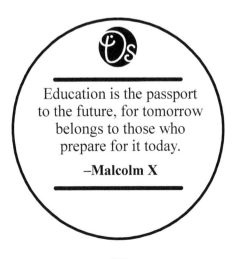

Education is the passport to the future, for tomorrow belongs to those who prepare for it today.

–Malcolm X

Self-Reflection: Studying and Maintaining a Strong GPA

- What are some of our biggest weaknesses with regard to studying?
- What are some ways you can study more effectively?
- Is it easier for you to study alone or with a group?

_____

_____

_____

_____

_____

_____

_____

_____

_____

_____

_____

_____

_____

_____

_____

_____

_____

_____

_____

_____

_____

_____

- Do you understand your college's GPA system?
- Have you struggled to maintain a high GPA in the past?
- How did you manage to improve or maintain a good GPA?

_____

_____

_____

_____

_____

_____

_____

_____

_____

_____

_____

_____

_____

_____

_____

_____

_____

_____

_____

_____

Student Life

If you enjoyed being a part of social groups in high school, you might also enjoy exploring opportunities for participating in social groups in college. Even if you don't consider yourself to be a "social butterfly", there might still be social groups in college that interest you.

Most social groups in college are formed by students based on shared interests, values, representations, ethnic or social background. For example, there are creative clubs such as theatre, art, and music. There are also social groups of various cultures and religions. It is also common for colleges and universities to have social groups that support the LGBT community and activism. For some colleges and universities, the list of social groups is endless.

How do you know if being involved in a social group is right for you? If you share the same interests as a particular group and you want to be actively involved or surround yourself with others with the same interest on a consistent basis, being involved in a social group might not be a bad idea. It's also a good way to meet new friends, especially if you're attending a college where you don't know anyone. If you're unsure about whether or not becoming a part of a social group or club is right for you, do your research. Read about their mission and cause if they have it listed on the college's website. If not, talk to members of the groups that interest you about their experience.

Sororities and Fraternities

Some of the most popular types of social groups in colleges across the United States are sororities and fraternities. Fraternities are typically composed of young men, while sororities are typically composed of young women. There are also co-ed organizations that refer to themselves as fraternities.

Fraternities and sororities typically promote their purpose as character development, leadership development or community building. Most sororities and fraternities have rituals and activities based on tradition and attract students who have common interest. Traditional emphasis in a specific religion or ethnic background is also common among sororities and fraternities. Some organizations put an emphasis on certain majors and are more of academic organizations than social.

Pros and Cons

Being a part of a fraternity or sorority comes with some benefits. Most of these organizations do provide opportunities for social and professional growth. They also provide a host of recreational activities, as well as opportunities for philanthropy. One of the biggest draws for these organizations are their networking opportunities.

Student members have the opportunity to network with one another on campus and with alumni. This provides opportunities for mentorship and even referrals for job opportunities when the time comes. Did you know there are currently more than nine million alumni of fraternities and sororities in the workforce across the country? That's a whole lot of networking!

If you're a "social butterfly", enjoy giving back, want to be engaged in the community, and are looking for personal growth, a fraternity or sorority might be a good choice for you.

However, there are some cons to consider. One of the most alarming drawbacks associated with these organizations is the practice of hazing. These are strenuous activities imposed on students who are seeking to become new members of a fraternity or sorority as part of their initiation or "training". Activities and rituals associated with hazing are often humiliating, physically exhausting and even dangerous.

Make sure that the organization you're looking to become a part of does not participate in hazing. Most colleges have policies against these types of practices for students' safety. However, it's worth talking to existing members of the organization of interest to get information about what really goes on behind the scenes. Again, hazing can be dangerous. Never engage in any activity that you know can put you in physical or academic jeopardy to gain the approval of a social group.

Joining these organizations also come with financial and time commitments. If you plan to reside in Greek housing or keep up with the ongoing activities, it won't come for free. You'll also need to make yourself available for certain activities and events throughout the year to remain active. This can become taxing if you already have a full schedule or have difficulty prioritizing your time.

Religion and Culture on Campus

Religion

It is not uncommon for students to suddenly feel uncomfortable with exercising or talking about their religion once they enter into college. This is because, unlike most students' home environment, several religions are encouraged on college campus, even groups of non-religion. This can be a bit of a culture shock and might easily make you uncomfortable with being open about your religion. However, you shouldn't be uncomfortable or afraid. In fact, most colleges have a variety of religious groups that you can connect with.

Most colleges also have policies that encourage the mutual respect of all religions. These policies are designed to encourage students to exercise their religion or explore that of others in a climate that is open and diverse. In many cases, the same is true for policies in the classroom with regard to discrimination against religion associated with course literature and assignments. These policies extend to religious-based clothing and accessories, and even distributing literature and flyers.

Culture

The culture of colleges and universities may vary based on demographics and mission. For example, a school with a population of majority white students might have a different culture than that of a Historically Black College in terms of activities, social groups and resources. The same may be true for students who are a part of the LGBT community.

Most colleges and universities have policies that encourage diversity and inclusion, regardless of race or sexual orientation. However, be sure to let someone know if you ever feel threatened or harassed by a group of students, as this could be potentially dangerous. Unfortunately, bullying does not stop in high school, despite school policies.

The good news is most schools have resources available to underrepresented minorities to make sure there is a network of support for all students, especially in instances of discrimination. Examples include counseling groups and multicultural clubs and departments. It is recommended that you read your school's policies on discrimination and available resources.

Residential Life

Student Housing

Living as a resident on campus comes with a lot excitement, change and responsibility. If you plan to reside in a dorm with shared living, you will need to become adjusted to living with others. Some might find this fun because they enjoy being in the company of others. However, if you have difficulty sharing your space with others, it might come with more of an adjustment.

There are many options for campus housing. For examples, many dorms offer single beds and multiple beds with the option for a private or shared bathroom. Communal amenities such as shared showers and sinks are also common, especially in freshman dorms. Campus apartments are also becoming increasingly popular. Most colleges restrict apartment space to upper classmen but some are more lenient. Apartment-style living typically includes multiple bedrooms, multiple bathrooms, a shared living room, kitchen, and laundry area.

Apartment-style living can be beneficial to students who would prefer to cook their own meals, rather than pay for a student meal plan which is offered by colleges with food and beverage facilities on campus. This set up also creates a shared living environment with more privacy and more space. However, the more space, the higher the cost.

Regardless of the style of campus living, you will be responsible for every day chores such as cleaning your living space and washing your laundry. You will also be responsible for your own meals if you don't have a meal plan.

Campus housing also comes with campus rules. For example, most campuses have curfews for underclassmen and codes of conduct. College dormitories also have what is called a Residence Hall Director to help assist with managing day to day operations. If you have questions about expectations, restrictions and rules, the Resident Hall Director is available to assist you.

If you plan to stay off campus or at home, it's still a good idea to practice handling the responsibilities of living on your own (i.e., cleaning and preparing meals) so that you're better prepared for life after college.

Most students choose to live with a roommate to save on the cost of living. If you plan to live with a roommate, here are a few tips to help you get off to a good start and maintain a good relationship:

- Introduce yourself as early as possible
- Get to know your roommate's likes and dislikes
- Establish mutual rules (i.e., no loud music when studying, cleaning common areas)
- Respect one another's space
- Keep your living area clean
- Never take any of your roommate's belongings without their permission
- Practice good hygiene
- Be courteous of one another

If you ever find yourself in an uncomfortable position with your roommate, and you're unsure about how to address it, talk to you Resident Hall Director.

Self-Reflection: Student Life—Social Groups, Sororities and Fraternities

- Were you involved in any social groups in high school or in your community?
- If so, what groups did you enjoy participating in most?
- Are there any groups at the college you plan to attend with similar activities and values?

_____

_____

_____

_____

_____

_____

_____

_____

_____

_____

_____

_____

_____

_____

_____

_____

_____

_____

- Are you interested in a sorority or fraternity?
- Why or why not?
- If you are interested, which organization appeals to you most?

_____

_____

_____

_____

_____

_____

_____

_____

_____

_____

_____

_____

_____

_____

_____

_____

_____

_____

Self-Reflection: Student Life—Religion and Culture

- What groups are on campus that support your religious beliefs?
- If there are none, how do you plan to seek religious support?

_____

_____

_____

_____

_____

_____

_____

_____

_____

_____

_____

_____

_____

_____

_____

_____

_____

_____

_____

_____

- Do you have any concerns about the culture of the college where you plan to attend?
- If so, what are they, and what resources available for support?

_____

_____

_____

_____

_____

_____

_____

_____

_____

_____

_____

_____

_____

_____

_____

_____

_____

_____

_____

_____

Self-Reflection: Student Life—Student Housing

- Do you plan to live in student housing?
- If so, what type/style of housing do you plan to live in?
- If you plan to have a roommate, what rules would you like to establish with them?

_____

_____

_____

_____

_____

_____

_____

_____

_____

_____

_____

_____

_____

_____

_____

_____

_____

_____

Little minds are tamed and subdued by misfortune; but great minds rise above it.

– Washington Irving

Dealing with Conflict

Throughout your time in college, you are bound to make great friends and have wonderful experiences. Unfortunately, you are also bound to experience conflict. However, it's important that you learn to deal with conflict effectively in order to be successful in college.

Conflict with Other Students

College can be a lot like high school in that there are students who form informal cliques and give other students a hard time. At some point, you might find yourself in a disagreement with another student based on varying opinions or a simple misunderstanding. For example, what if a roommate borrows something but doesn't return it? What if you learn that a friend has been talking about you behind your back? What if you discover someone took something from your bedroom that belonged to you? What if someone calls you out of your name or constantly harasses you?

It can be hard to deal with people who make you feel hurt or disrespected. Unfortunately, you don't have control over other people's actions. However, you do have control of your own! It's important that you don't allow yourself to act out of character when conflict arises. Doing so will only make the conflict worse. The best thing for you to do is remain calm and identify possible solutions to help resolve the conflict.

Start by being clear on what the conflict is and having a conversation with the person involved. Ask clarifying questions and make statements of concern, rather than making accusations or being confrontational. Remain calm, take deep breathes, try not to raise your voice, and refrain from interrupting the other person while they're speaking.

Based on the information you're able to gather during your attempt to address the conflict, you can decide whether or not you want to continue to associate with the person involved, or if it's necessary to take further action. For instance, if in the example where a roommate borrows something without returning it, the roommate apologizes after you bring it to their attention and does not make it a habit, consider the problem resolved. However, if the problem persists, even after addressing it, you might need to involve the Resident Hall Director.

Some conflicts can be dangerous and should not be handled alone. For example, constant bullying or harassment should never be tolerated and warrants the attention of a college official or counselor. If the person causing the conflict is making threats, you should involve campus police. Never engage in a physical altercation with anyone on or off campus. Doing so can result in bodily injury to yourself and the other person involved. It can also result in academic probation, expulsion or worse—criminal charges.

Conflict with Professors

Sometimes students find themselves in conflict with their professors. This might be because the student disagrees with a professor's teaching methods, expectations or an assigned grade. It could even be the result of something as simple as a personality clash. Colleges have codes of conduct for professors that would prevent most conflicting situations to arise between them and their students. However, if you ever feel harassed or treated unequally by a professor, be sure to bring it to the attention of a college official.

If you are in conflict with a professor over a grade or assignment, take the time to talk to the professor about your concerns, ask clarifying questions and identify possible solutions. Let your professors know that you value their expertise and want to do well in their courses. Most importantly, you want to work together to improve your relationship and academic performance.

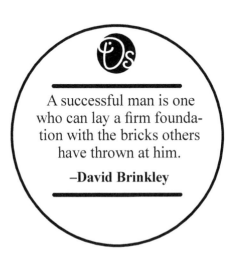

A successful man is one who can lay a firm foundation with the bricks others have thrown at him.

–David Brinkley

Self-Reflection: Dealing with Conflict

- Have you had trouble dealing with conflict in the past?
- If so, what can you do to practice handling conflict appropriately as a college student?

_____

_____

_____

_____

_____

_____

_____

_____

_____

_____

_____

_____

_____

_____

_____

_____

_____

_____

_____

_____

- Describe the conversation you would have with your professor if you were in conflict about a grade or assignment.

_____

_____

_____

_____

_____

_____

_____

_____

_____

_____

_____

_____

_____

_____

_____

_____

_____

_____

_____

_____

_____

_____

_____

Safety

Maintaining your safety is just as important as maintaining good grades while in college. It might sound cliché, but it's important to put safety first in everything you do. This is especially true now that you'll be on your own without anyone to keep an eye out on you, protect you or hold you accountable. Though there is a sense of freedom that comes along with this, there are also several dangers—some which you can afflict upon yourself, and some which can be afflicted upon you by others.

Creating a Safe Environment

While on campus, lock the doors to your dorm room or apartment when you're away. You should also lock the doors of your vehicle if you plan to have one on campus.

If you're taking night classes, try finding someone to walk with you to and from class, especially if your class is a considerable distance from your dorm or apartment. Unfortunately, criminals tend to prey on those who they think are vulnerable. College-aged students certainly fit this description because they are young and, in many cases, away from home. Common acts of crime on or near college campuses include theft and sexual assault. Walking with someone can help prevent this from happening.

Never invite anyone into your dorm or apartment who you don't know. If you meet someone you'd like to study with or who you simply want to get to know, invite them to meet you in a common space like the library or the campus quad.

Colleges also have safety and security measures in place to help keep you safe. For example, Campus Police is available to students and ready to respond in the event that they run into trouble or notice anything suspicious. Colleges also put rules and procedures in place to protect the safety of their students, including evacuation plans for emergencies—fire, weather threats or active shooter.

Be sure to keep the number to the Campus Police handy at all times and review your college's evacuation plans and safety procedures. If you ever find yourself in a situation that needs immediate attention—safety, medical or otherwise, call 911 immediately.

Partying and Drinking

The concept of partying and drinking is very exciting for many students because it gives them a sense of fun and adventure. However, this can also be very dangerous. Whether you're partying on or off campus, avoid alcohol at all costs. Remember, the legal age for drinking is 21. Indulging in alcohol before then is considered drinking underage and is illegal.

Drinking alcohol can impair your mobility and ability to make sound decisions. This can cause you to have a damaging fall or worse—make you an easy target for sexual assault. Even when drinking a non-alcoholic beverage, you should never drink anything that you didn't see prepared or that you walked away from. Your eyes should remain on your beverage at all times. It is not uncommon for people to drug a drink while no one's watching.

Driving while drinking is also incredibly dangerous, no matter how few drinks you've had. If you plan to attend a party where you know drinking will be taking place, make sure there is a designated driver.

Drinking can lead to brain damage, which can cause memory loss or the loss of motor skills. Liver and other chronic diseases can also develop over time. Young adults who begin drinking before the age of 21 are more likely to develop alcohol addiction, which increases their chances of chronic illness and premature death.

Some students aren't into the party scene but use alcohol to distract them from unwanted emotions (or to "take the edge off"). However, alcohol is only a temporary distraction and only leads to dependency. The last thing you want to depend on to get through college is alcohol because it will actually take away from your focus, which is what you'll need most. Furthermore, dependency can lead to addiction.

Drugs

Drugs should also be avoided at all costs. Like alcohol, they can also inhibit normal brain function, prevent the ability to make rational decisions and lead to death.

There's no such thing as a safe drug. One of the most common traps that college students fall into is believing that a drug isn't harmful because of its trendy name, or that one drug is less harmful than another, especially if everybody seems to be doing it. However, the fact is, all drugs are dangerous, no matter the type or how large or small the amount. Even smoking cigarettes is a gateway to other drugs because it introduces your body to nicotine and leads to dependency. Drugs affect what's called the limbic system by causing dangerously large amounts of dopamine to flood the system. This causes a shift in the way the brain functions and can prevent you from thinking clearly. Drug use can also lead to lung and heart disease overtime.

No matter how harmless a drug might appear to be, there is no way to know what you're actually consuming. For example, marijuana, which has negative effects of its own, can have even worse effects if laced with other lethal drugs, such as cocaine. Drugs don't come with instructions, ingredients or warning labels. There's simply no way of knowing what you're actually putting into your body. Some drugs are made of deadly chemicals that can send you into a coma or cause your heart to stop immediately upon taking them. Trying a drug of any kind can be deadly.

Prescription drugs are no exception. Another dangerous misconception is that taking a prescription drugs is safer than taking drugs that aren't prescribed by a doctor. This is false! Even drugs prescribed by a doctor can be dangerous if the drug was not originally prescribed for the person consuming them, or if it's not taken according to the doctor's orders. Students are increasingly overdosing on opioids (pain pills) that have been prescribed to a family member or a friend. Opioids are thought to "take the edge off" or numb pain since they are created as pain killers. However, improper dosage of these drugs can lead to immediate death.

Communicate Your Whereabouts

Always make sure that someone knows where you are and who you are with when leaving campus. If you turn up missing, someone needs to know where you were last and who was with you in order to track you down and come to your rescue. Simply let a friend or family member know where you plan to go, the name of the person who will be accompanying you, and what time you expect to return. You should also keep your phone charged at all times so that you can reach out to someone in the event of an emergency.

All progress takes place outside of your comfort zone.

–Michael John Bobak

Self-Reflection: Safety

- What are some safety measures you can put in place while attending college?

_____

_____

_____

_____

_____

_____

_____

_____

_____

_____

_____

_____

_____

_____

_____

_____

_____

_____

_____

_____

_____

_____

- How well do you handle peer pressure?
- How can you avoid being pressured into trying harmful substances while in college?

_____

_____

_____

_____

_____

_____

_____

_____

_____

_____

_____

_____

_____

_____

_____

_____

_____

_____

_____

_____

_____

_____

Our greatest fear should not be of failure, but of succeeding at things in life that don't really matter.

–Francis Chan

Dating, Love and Sex

If you haven't already begun dating, there will be plenty of opportunity to do so in college. The challenge is balancing dating and college life and keeping your priorities in order. Remember, you're going to college to complete a degree, not to find love. Although, it's not unheard of to find love in college.

Dating

If you're planning to date in college, make sure you're clear on what dating means to you and the person you're dating. Dating is all about getting to know someone over time so that, eventually, you can decide if a person is someone you'd like to enter into a long-term relationship with. Going out on a date with someone does not mean that you have to be committed to the person forever. It simply means you're interested in getting to know more about the other person—their background, interests, likes and dislikes. It's also a great opportunity to explore what you have in common.

Many people use "dating" and "committed relationships" interchangeably. However, the two should not be confused. Dating is the "getting to know you" phase, whereas a committed relationship is the "we're seeing each other and no one else" phase. A committed relationship might also be solidified by giving each other titles, such as "boyfriend" and "girlfriend".

Unlike a casual dating relationship, a committed relationship is one where two people decide to remain in a relationship with just each other. At this point, they both feel they've gathered all the information they need to assure that they have shared interests, love one another, and see a future together long-term. In most cases, couples who enter into a committed relationship have an ultimate goal of marriage.

The best thing you can do is to take time to get to know yourself as you continue to mature before trying to fully commit to someone else. Start by simply getting to know the person you might be interested in as friends and spending quality time with them. If you're interested in dating but it makes you uncomfortable at first, try double-dating with friends. Date in public spaces and not in your dorm or at someone else's apartment alone so that you're not tempted to have sex prematurely. This is also a good safety precaution if you're dating someone you don't already know. Always let someone know where you are and who you're with, especially if you're planning to date off campus.

Love vs. Sex

As a young adult, it can be very easy to confuse love with emotions that are driven by hormones. For example, you might be talking to or spending time with someone who you really like, and feel nervous or become excited when you see them or hear their voice. You might even find yourself thinking about the person often when they're not around.

This might simply mean you're very attracted to the other person, not that you're in love. Some refer to this as "puppy love"—a phrase people use to describe emotions that mimic love during an early stage of a relationship.

Love is having a deep affection for someone that comes naturally and is unconditional. Love is much like oxygen. We all need it to survive. Oxygen comes to us naturally. We don't have to create it. Oxygen is always available to us, whether we're up, down, right or wrong. Oxygen is available to us unconditionally and is everlasting. It gives without ever expecting anything in return.

If you're unable to love someone in this fashion, you still have some growing to do before you can proclaim that you're actually in love. If you genuinely develop feelings for someone while dating, whether you love them or care deeply for them, and that person hurts you, it's normal to experience feelings of sadness and even anger. Some refer to this as "heartbreak". However, never find fault in yourself for someone's else's irresponsible actions.

If you have difficulty getting past the hurt that someone has caused you, focus on things they love to do, rather than spending time replaying what went wrong or trying to figure out what could have been done differently. You might not ever forget, but eventually, you'll get past your feelings of hurt. Make a conscious decision to let go. The more you hold you're your hurt or anger, the harder it will be for you to move past it. If you find yourself consumed with feelings of sadness, and have great difficulty focusing on anything else, talk to a professional to make sure your you are not suffering from depression.

Introducing sex into a dating relationship is never a good idea. Sex can produce hormones that send bonding signals to the brain. This can make it difficult for you to distinguish between whether what you're experiencing is love or lust. Never let anyone convince you to have sex with them to prove you love them. If someone really loves you, they wouldn't pressure you to do anything you're uncomfortable with doing.

Being pressured to have sex is never ok, neither are emotional or physical abuse. In fact, these are completely selfish acts, which is the opposite of love. If you ever feel pressured or abused in any way, you should distance yourself from the person and let someone know right away.

Sex is not a recreational sport. Dating or not, sex might seem like nothing more than a fun pass-time while in college. However, sex is not just about fun and games. It's a form of bonding that has long-lasting effects. Did you know that your brain actually releases a chemical called oxytocin when having sex, which is the same chemical released when mothers breastfeed their babies to help them bond? That's how powerful oxytocin is. So, the idea that you can just have sex for the fun of it is completely false! It's a lot more complicated than that.

Sex has emotional effects. It can be rather hard to emotionally distance yourself from someone you've had sex with. What you think might be fun or lead to love could actually leave you feeling rejected and empty in the long run. These feelings can ultimately harm your self-esteem.

Sexually Transmitted Diseases (STDs)

Beyond emotional discourse, casual sex increases your risk of contracting STDs. The most common forms of STDs are chlamydia, gonorrhea, genital herpes, human papillomavirus (HPV), syphilis and HIV. Although chlamydia and gonorrhea are treatable, they aren't treated overnight, and can have long-term effects later in adulthood. Both of these infections can cause unpleasant orders, discharges, and lots of itching and swelling. Over time, these infections can lead to cervical cancer in women or complications with becoming pregnant. It can also lead to sterilization in men. HIV and genital herpes are not curable. If you contract these viruses, they will remain with you for a lifetime.

No form of sexual activity or protection is 100% safe. Don't be convinced that you're safe from these STDs by using protection (i.e., condoms) or that engaging in other forms of sex, such as oral sex, is safer. STDs are spread through the exchange of bodily fluid, and oral sex certainly does not exclude this type of exchange. Likewise, condoms are not 100% guaranteed to prevent leakage of bodily fluid.

Bodily fluid isn't the only thing to be concerned about. Genital herpes can be contracted simply through skin to skin contact—no fluid necessary. So, think twice before deciding to engage in any type of sexual activity.

Unplanned Pregnancy

Aside from contracting a STD, having sex can lead to an unplanned pregnancy. Having a baby while in college can be incredibly challenging. The responsibility of taking care of a baby and meeting the demands of coursework can be overwhelming and distract from your duties as both a parent and a student. This can lead to extremely high levels of stress. It is not uncommon for young women in college to delay their college education after becoming pregnant. Young men can also find it very difficult to maintain a normal college schedule while working to support a child.

If you might already be pregnant or think you've impregnated someone, talk to someone you trust and seek help from a medical physician right away. Pregnancy can affect your emotions and health, and the health of the baby, so it's important to have a strong support system.

Self-Reflection:
Dating, Love and Sex

- Do you plan to date while in college?
- If so, what are you looking for in a dating relationship?

_____

_____

_____

_____

_____

_____

_____

_____

_____

_____

_____

_____

_____

_____

_____

_____

_____

_____

_____

_____

_____

_____

- How do you plan to manage dating and your college responsibilities?

_____

_____

_____

_____

_____

_____

_____

_____

_____

_____

_____

_____

_____

_____

_____

_____

_____

_____

_____

_____

Coping with Stress And Mental Illness

According to mental health research conducted by the National Alliance on Mental Illness (NAMI), one in four students have a diagnosable mental illness. Of those, 40% do not seek help. Beyond mental illness, stress and anxiety or very prevalent among college students. This is in large part due to the overwhelming responsibility that comes with being a college student. For example, it's not uncommon for students to feel overwhelmed by coursework or anxious about being away from home.

It is important that you learn to manage stress and use preventive measures to avoid stress. It is equally as important that you recognize mental illness and manage it appropriately so that you are successful in your college career and in achieving your life goals.

Physical Health and Nutrition

A healthy diet and exercise are key to minimizing stress. College life can become so busy that you forget to take care of yourself. All-day classes and late-night studying can make it hard to maintain a balanced diet. Quick snacks might seem convenient, but it's important to maintain a healthy diet so that you have the natural energy you need to keep up with your busy schedule and maintain the focus you need to be successful. A poor diet can result in a lack of energy, lack of focus, and contribute to stress. It can also lead to bad health, including obesity, diabetes, high cholesterol and high blood pressure. Eat foods that are high in nutrition, such as vegetables, fruit, whole grain and protein. Try to avoid foods that are high in sugar and calories, and low in nutritional value. Never attempt a "fad" diet or try any dietary supplements in an attempt to stay healthy without first consulting with your physician.

Daily exercise is also important to your physical and mental health. It is recommended that you engage in moderate exercise for at least 30 minutes a day. Most colleges have a gym and provide fitness classes. If you feel you need a little encouragement to remain physically active, it might be a good idea to join a fitness club or class.

Another important component of maintaining your physical and mental health is getting enough rest. Your body needs anywhere between 6 to 8 hours of sleep per day. Depriving your body of the rest it needs only adds to your levels of stress and diminishes your ability to focus.

Eating Disorders and Addiction

Millions of college students develop eating disorders during their college years. This is true of both young women and young men. Eating disorders involve extreme behaviors concerning food, and involve eating habits and weight perceptions that are unhealthy and can be life-threatening. Stress can cause students to overeat and attempt to reverse it by regurgitating it, which is also known as binge eating or bulimia.

Some students also become obsessed with their image and the idea of remaining extremely thin. They become extremely fearful of gaining weight and limit their food intake in a way that is so extreme, they don't take in enough calories to support a healthy body weight. This condition is also known as anorexia.

Binge eating disorder—constant cravings that occur throughout the day—is also associated with poor body image and low self-esteem. Over-exercising is also a symptom of these disorders. This behavior often leads to addiction and, if left untreated, can be deadly. These disorders can lead to irregular heartbeats, distorted body image, kidney failure, stunted growth and heart problems. According to statistics provided by the National Association of Anorexia Nervosa and Associated Disorders (ANAD), one person dies as a direct result of an eating disorder every 62 minutes.

If you ever struggle with symptoms of an eating disorder, talk to someone you trust and seek help from a healthcare professional. You can also visit nationaleatingdisorders.org or eatingdisorderhope.com for free resources and tools.

Anxiety

It is natural for you to experience some level of anxiety, especially as a college student. For example, you might feel anxious before an exam or about meeting someone for the first time. However, if you consistently experience high levels of anxiety, and it prevents you from functioning normally as a result of fear and stress, you might be suffering from an anxiety disorder. According to the Anxiety and Depression Association of America (ADAA), anxiety disorders affect 40 million adults over the age of 18, and 75% of those affected by an anxiety disorder will experience their first episode before the age of 22. Anxiety disorder is much more common than you might think, which is why it's important to understand and recognize symptoms.

Panic disorders come with extreme phases of panic, often coupled with shortness of breath, dizziness, rapid heartbeat, diarrhea and nausea. Some people suffer from obsessive compulsive disorder (ODC), which is a type of anxiety that causes people to obsess over or indulge in behavior that might be completely irrational. For example, constantly re-sharpening pencils that are already perfectly sharpened or reorganizing things that are already perfectly organized are signs of OCD.

Post trauma stress disorder (PTSD) is also a common form of anxiety. Young adults with PTSD might experience random flashbacks, feelings of fear, sweating and loss of breath after being triggered by something that causes feelings of a traumatic experience to resurface. Random reminders of the incident that trigger the senses (i.e., sight, smell, sound or touch) and high levels of stress can often times lead to PTSD symptoms.

If you ever struggle with symptoms of anxiety, talk to someone you trust and seek help from a healthcare professional. You can also visit ulifeline.org or the Anxiety and Depression Association of America at adaa.org for free resources and tools.

ADHD

If you've been diagnosed with Attention Deficit Hyperactivity Disorder (ADHD), you're already familiar with the challenges of staying focused and organized. However, many students struggle with ADHD without ever having been diagnosed. ADHD is pattern of inattention and/or hyperactivity-impulsivity, caused by imbalanced chemicals in the brain that interfere with every day functioning. Much like anxiety, every one experiences the inability to focus from time to time. For example, if you're stressed about something that is taking place in your life, you might not be able to focus on studying.

However, if you're consistently unable to focus while studying, find it hard to sit still in your classes or feel the impulse to jump up and move around during classes, you might be suffering from ADHD. If you suspect you might be struggling with ADHD or have already been diagnosed, reach out to a clinical healthcare provider regarding a comprehensive clinical assessment and to obtain available resources.

Helpful tips to keep in mind include using planners and apps to stay organized, channeling energy through exercise, such as taking short walks in between classes, and eliminating things that cause you to be easily distracted. You should also talk to your professor about extended time for assignments and exams. Useful online resources include the Attention Deficit Disorder Organization at add.org or adhdadult.com

Depression and Suicide

Depression is very common among college students. Though the topic might seem "taboo", it's important to understand what it means and seek help if you notice symptoms. Feelings of sadness are normal. However, if you find yourself feeling constantly hopeless or helpless and isolated from everything and everyone around you, you might be suffering from depression.

Depression is a disorder of the brain caused by a combination of genetics, biological, psychological and environmental factors. It causes constant feelings of sadness and hopelessness that cause you to be disinterested in things you once enjoyed, lose interest in being around friends and family, and lose interest in life in general. It can also interfere with everyday functions, such as eating and sleeping. As a college student, depression could interfere with your ability to study, concentrate, set goals, or establish a social life.

Depression is the number one reason students drop out of school, and can lead to thoughts of suicide if left untreated. If you experience loss of appetite, constant sadness, feelings of hopelessness, trouble sleeping (or having only an interest in sleeping), talk to someone you trust and seek help from a healthcare provider.

It's important that you seek help, even if you're unsure about whether or not depression is what you're experiencing. Undiagnosed depression can spiral out of control fast, so it's not worth the risk. Don't try to self-diagnose yourself and "fix it" on your own. It's better to seek professional help before the condition spirals out of control. Don't be embarrassed or afraid. There are many trained professionals who are trained and ready to meet you right where you are.

If you ever have suicidal thoughts, contact someone right away! The National Suicide Hotline is a great resource that is available to you with trained professionals who are ready to help 24 hours a day at **1-800-273-8255.**

If a friend or peer shares with you that they are contemplating suicide or you suspect that they're contemplating doing so because of verbal references or changes in behavior, contact someone right away! Other useful resources include ulifeline.org and The American College Health Association – acha.org.

Things to Consider When Managing a Mental Illness

If you've been diagnosed with a mental illness, consider attending college close to home and your medical service providers. If you plan to attend college away from home, make sure you arrange the proper medical services, including the maintenance of health insurance. You should also identify a healthcare provider and pharmacy for any necessary prescriptions. Once you identify a healthcare provider, work with them to develop a plan for monitoring your symptoms and establishing a routine for maintenance of your condition.

Choosing small classes with small ratios can also be helpful, as it can provide more of the individual attention you might need and eliminate the distraction of a crowded classroom. Talk to housing services about any special accommodations you might need if you plan to live on campus.

Most importantly, become familiar with your college's Clinical Services Department and available resources, as well as the resources available in the community. College counselors can help you find a long-term therapist or doctor in the community.

If you have a mental health diagnosis or learning disability and attend a public school, you have been entitled to special education services under the Individuals with Disabilities Education Act (IDEA). Upon graduation, you'll be leaving your IEP (Individualized Education Program) behind and entering into your college's particular system for accommodating disabilities.

The Americans with Disabilities Act requires colleges to make "reasonable accommodations" to help you succeed, but you and your parents will now be responsible for planning your own "IEP." Contact the college's disability resource center about any necessary documentation or special accommodations you might need.

Self-Reflection: Coping with Stress and Mental Illness

- What are things you've done to cope with stress in the past that can continue to help you while in college?

_____

_____

_____

_____

_____

_____

_____

_____

_____

_____

_____

_____

_____

_____

_____

_____

_____

_____

_____

_____

_____

- Have you been diagnosed with a mental health disorder or experienced symptoms of a disorder?
- If so, how do you plan to maintain your mental health while in college?
- If not, what are signs you should watch for—from yourself and those around you—as indicators of a mental health disorder?

_____

_____

_____

_____

_____

_____

_____

_____

_____

_____

_____

_____

_____

_____

_____

_____

_____

_____

Balancing College Life and Work

Many students secure a part-time job to help pay their way through college. Some even work full-time jobs and attend night classes to make ends meet. Whether you're working full-time or part-time, balancing school and work can be critical to your academic success.

If you plan to work while attending school, consider the number of hours you can work in comparison to the number of classes you're scheduled to take and the amount of time you'll need to dedicate to studying. If you have no option but to work longer hours, you might consider only taking a few courses at a time or taking some courses online at your own pace.

It's a good idea to determine how much money you'll actually need every month before taking on a job with a set number of hours. This will help you to determine how many hours you need to work to support yourself. It's also a good idea to talk to your employer about flexible hours. Depending on the demands of the job, some employers will allow flexible hours to help accommodate your college schedule.

Most colleges have student jobs available on campus. If you're planning to live on campus, taking on a student job is worth considering, as it is a convenient way to work part-time and maintain your studies. Working off campus comes with the added responsibility of commuting back and forth.

Plan ahead and take time off when necessary. Review your work schedule for conflicts with any scheduled exams or other important school events. Work with your manager to rearrange your schedule accordingly or take time off.

Between work, class and studying, you might not have time for much else, so try not to overdo it. Having a social life is important, and so is spending time with friends, but be careful not to spend so much time on your social life that you don't get enough rest and you're easily burned out.

Success is the sum of small efforts, repeated day-in and day-out.

–Robert Collier

Self-Reflection: Balancing College Life and Work

- Do you plan to work while in college?
- If so, what is the maximum number of hours you plan to work per day?
- What methods or tools can you use to help keep yourself organized?

Most of the important things in the world have been accomplished by people who have kept on trying when there seemed to be no help at all.

–Dale Carnegie

Saving Money

It can be very tempting to spend money unnecessarily while in college. A new sense of freedom combined with income from a part-time job makes spending appear to be a reasonable thing to do. However, if you're not careful, you can spend all of your income prematurely and still have a deficit for the things you really need (i.e., books, food, gas).

Even if you're not working, credit card debt is also a common issue for college students. Applying for a credit card seems easy enough, but maintaining payments on the balance can be challenging, especially for a college student without a high paying job. Unfortunately, many college students fall into the trap of charging everything onto a credit card and defaulting on their balance. This, in turn, ruins their credit. Having good credit is important for making major purchases in the future, such as a home or vehicle. A good credit score indicates to creditors (or lenders) that you have the ability to pay back what you borrow based on the amount of debt you have and your payment history. You don't want to ruin your credit score before getting out into the real world.

So, how can you avoid this trap and start saving? You can start by not spending money on things unnecessarily. For example, use the coffee machine on campus to brew coffee, rather than purchasing your coffee from a coffee shop every day. Don't eat out every day— fast food runs can add up. Instead, purchase enough food items for the week and limit your fast food or restaurant purchases to once a week.

Don't shop for clothes unnecessarily. Purchase the bare essentials for your wardrobe and limit the purchase of "special attire" to just a few pieces.

If you have a car, don't waste your gas driving around to unnecessary places. Take advantage of the college shuttle or public transportation when possible. Create a social life that doesn't always cost you money. Limit your spending on club and party covers. You can also limit spending on recreational activities (i.e., movie theatres, bowling) to a few times a month, rather than every weekend.

Create a budget and set a goal for how much money you want to save each month. Categorize your expenses and keep track of your spending in each category, including your savings. This will help you to monitor where you're doing well and where you're overspending so that you can cut back or reevaluate your budget.

Open a savings account separate from your checking account and commit to leaving what goes into your savings untouched. This will help to keep you accountable for the savings goal you've set for yourself.

Self-Reflection: Saving Money

- What are some things you can cut back on while in college to save money?

_____

_____

_____

_____

_____

_____

_____

_____

_____

_____

_____

_____

_____

_____

_____

_____

_____

- What is your monthly budget?
- How much would you like to save each month?
- (If you haven't done so already, open a savings account).

Internships and Finding Jobs After College

The thought of finding a job after college can be exciting and intimidating at the same time. However, there are several steps you can take to help make your search a lot less stressful. The first thing to keep in mind is that it's never too early to start looking. Research companies and organizations that you'd like to work for based on your interests. Look for volunteer or internship opportunities at these companies so that you can get to know the staff and get a better feel for the work and culture. This is a great way to gain experience and begin building a relationship with those who you might potentially be working for if you decide to apply. Internships can also help to build your resume.

You can seek volunteer opportunities by visiting most companies' websites or contacting their human resources department. You should also talk to the Career Services staff at your college about internship opportunities that are available to you as a student. Career Services is available to help you identify possible career paths based on your declared major, and assist you identifying available job listings as the time draws nearer for graduation.

Talk to as many people as you know in the field that you're interested in and allow them to mentor you, if possible. This is also a great way to network. The more you connect with people with similar interests and experience, the more you establish exposure and support. Mentors can also provide letters of recommendations or great references, which are required by most companies looking to hire. Most times, college professors will also provide letter of recommendations for students who excel in their courses.

Social media is another way to connect with companies looking to hire. Follow the social media groups of the companies that interest you, stay engaged, and be on the lookout for job opportunities.

When applying for jobs, don't limit yourself to one application. Apply to several jobs that interest you. Most importantly, don't be discouraged when you receive a "no" from a company or no response at all. Remain persistent in your search. The right job is out there, you just need to stay the course!

Self-Reflection: Finding Internships and Jobs After College

- Describe your dream job.
- What type of company would you be interested in working for?

_____

_____

_____

_____

_____

_____

_____

_____

_____

_____

_____

_____

_____

_____

_____

_____

_____

_____

_____

_____

_____

_____

- Make a list of professionals you already know in your field of interest.
- If you don't yet know any professionals, describe what you plan to look for in a mentor.

_____

_____

_____

_____

_____

_____

_____

_____

_____

_____

_____

_____

_____

_____

_____

_____

_____

_____

_____

_____

_____

_____

Affirmational Thoughts and Next Steps

- Now that you've completed this book, write down some positive thoughts you have about your journey as a college student.
- What are you feeling more confident or optimistic about?

- What are your biggest takeaways?
- Place a sticky note on the pages that correlate with these takeaways as a reminder that you have a resource handy if a similar situation presents itself.

_____

_____

_____

_____

_____

_____

_____

_____

There is no secret to success. It is the result of preparation, hard work, and learning from failure.

–General Colin Powell

Let's Connect

Join Dr. Stem on Face Book Live on Tuesday evenings for discussions on topics discussed in this book and more.

Enroll in Parent & Teen Empowerment Webinars and online courses, and connect with other teenagers around the world for moral support, fun and encouragement.

All online programs are on: https://www.drstemmie.com/

Look out for the Parent & Teen Empowerment Conference or Workshop coming to your city, a city near you or at sea. Inquire at drstem14@gmail.com

About the Author

Originally from Zimbabwe, Africa, Dr. Sithembile "Stem" Mahlatini is president and owner of Global Counseling & Coaching Services, in Orlando, Florida, and she is also president and founder of Parent & Teen Empowerment Conference & Parent & Teen Empowerment Seminars. She is a certified life-career coach, author, licensed psychotherapist and motivational/inspirational speaker. She resides in Orlando, Florida USA.

Dr. Stem's life's work is to inspire, motivate and educate others through her books, seminars, workshops, and Counseling and Coaching Services. Drawing on her background as a licensed psychotherapist, life- career coach, speaker and author, she offers people practical advice on how to tap into their limitless power to change their lives, overcome roadblocks and aspire to be better than the circumstances that surround them. Her life-long goal is to continue to empower and inspire teenagers, parents, and couples to be winners at home, work and business. Her motto is, "Each day is an opportunity to change your life and bring out the new you."

Dr. Mahlatini attended Nova Southeastern University where she earned a doctorate degree in education, specializing in organizational leadership. She is also a graduate of Boston University, where she earned a master's degree in social work, and she is licensed as a psychotherapist in Massachusetts and Florida. She is a member of the Back Talk Toastmasters club, the Professional Woman Network, and the National Association of Social Workers.

Listen to DrStem weekly on The DrStem Show on https://americaoutloud.com/show/the-drstem-show/

Watch DrStem on The DrStem Show on Youtube for inspiration, encouragement and motivation through the interviews she conducts on the show, https://www.youtube.com/results?search_query=drstem+show

In addition to speaking and training, she counsels and coaches clients in her private practice offices in Altamonte Springs, Skype and telephonically. She serves clientele throughout the United States, Africa, the Caribbean, the United Kingdom, and Australia through one-on-one telephone coaching services.

Motivation is what gets you started. Habit is what keeps you going.

–Jim Ryun

Dr. Stem is available as a trainer and speaker for onsite trainings, groups, and one-on-one coaching for parents, teenagers, women and organizations. Consultations are conducted by telephone or on-site. Her programs include:

- Bridging the Gap Between Parents and Teenagers
- Pampering The "Princess Within"
- Overcoming Being All Things to All People
- Possibilities – Turning Dreams into Reality
- Free at Last – Setting Boundaries
- How to Deal with Toxic People
- 15 Strategies to Achieve Your Dream
- How to Live a Simpler Life
- Living a New Life of Confidence-Developing A Healthy Self Esteem
- Taking Charge of Your Life, Money and Family
- Change Your Thinking – Change Your Life
- The Rollercoaster Ride Is Over! Handling Emotions
- Handling Stress: Sink, Swim or Float & More

Book Dr. Stem Mahlatini as your next motivational/inspirational speaker for your women's retreat, church, youth retreat, seminar, school assembly, or Business Management–Employee event.

Training, Individual and Group Life Coaching

Contact Dr. Stem Mahlatini at:
PHONE: (781) 254-1602

Dr. Stem authored/co-authored the following titles:

1. Beyond the Tears-Bruised but Not Broken-Author Biography-A story of Hope & Encouragement
2. The Power of Prayer & Belief
3. It's Time to Shift -From Fear to Faith
4. Finding Your True Self
5. Emotional Wellness for Women vol. 1
6. Emotional Wellness for Women vol. II
7. Emotional Wellness for Women vol. III
8. The Baby Boomer's Handbook for Women
9. The Power of God
10. Celebration of Life-Inspiration for Women
11. How to Survive When Your Ship Is Sinking: Weathering Life's Storms
12. Beyond the Scars: Real Life Accounts for Women Who Overcame Adversity
13. Confident not Corky: Why self-esteem is Key to a Successful Life, Business and Career
14. Unstoppable: A woman's Guide to Self-confidence book and workbook.
15. Zero Limits: A Teenager's Guide to Life's choices